ISLAM

Khadijah Knight

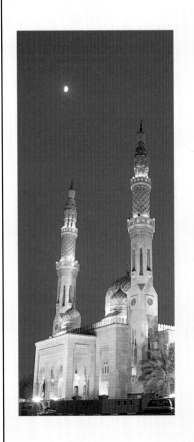

Wayland

For Abu Ahmad
who knows that what counts
is not where you start but
where you finish.

First published in 1995 by
Wayland (Publishers) Ltd,
61 Western Road, Hove,
East Sussex BN3 1JD

Copyright © Wayland (Publishers) Ltd, 1995

This book was prepared for Wayland (Publishers) Ltd
by Ruth Nason

Khadijah Knight asserts her right to be identified
as author of this work, in accordance with the
Copyright, Designs and Patents Act 1988

Book design: Alex Latham, Ken Alston

Typeset: A.J. Latham Ltd,
Houghton Regis, Dunstable, Bedfordshire

Printed and bound in Italy by G. Canale & C.S.p.A., Turin

British Library Cataloguing in Publication Data
Knight, Khadijah
    Islam. – (World Religions Series)
    I. Title. II. Series
    297

    ISBN 0-7502-1445-7

*Cover: This boy from
Bukhara, Uzbekistan,
is keeping alive the
traditions of Islamic
scholarship by studying
the Qur'an.*
*Page 1: Jumeira, Dubai,
mosque at night.*
*Page 3: Even little
children join in the Id
prayer in Cairo, Egypt.*

Acknowledgements

Thanks to everyone at Islamic Consultancy and Information
Services, P.O. Box 2842, London W6 9ZH (Tel. 0181 748 2424)
and at Islamic Consultancy and Information Services of Scotland,
127 Cumbernauld Road, Stepps, Glasgow G33 6EY (Tel. 0141
779 1801).

The author and publishers thank the following for their permission
to reproduce photographs: Guy Hall: p. 38 (top); Christine
Osborne: cover, pp. 3, 24, 27, 34; TRIP: pp. 1 (H. Rogers), 4, 5
(top) (Joan Wakelin), 5 (bottom) (S. Hill), 6, 7 (J. Kilby), 9
(J. Kilby), 10 (top) (H. Rogers), 10 (bottom) (A. Gamiet), 12, 15
(H. Rogers), 17, 18 (M. Barlow), 19 (top), 19 (bottom)
(A. Gamiet), 22 (C. Rennie), 23 (F. Good), 25, 28 (H. Rogers),
29, 31 (H. Rogers), 32, 33 (top) (W. Jacobs), 33 (bottom), 35
(H. Rogers), 37 (M. Lines), 38 (bottom), 39, 40 (top), 40
(bottom) (C. Rennie), 41, 45 (top) (H. Rogers), 45 (bottom).

Contents

Every time a Muslim mentions Muhammad, he or she adds 'Salla-llahu alaihi wa sallam' ('Peace and blessings of Allah upon him'). In print, these Arabic words are expressed by this logotype: ﷺ.

After the names of all the Prophets and the names of the twelve Shi'ah Imams (see page 11), Muslims add 'Peace be upon him'. These words in Arabic, 'Alaihi salaam', are represented by the logotype ﵊.

INTRODUCTION

Islam is the faith and way of life of more than a thousand million people around the world. These followers of Islam are called Muslims, and the basic belief that they declare is that 'There is no god except Allah and Muhammad is the Messenger of Allah'. These words are called the 'Shahadah'.

To help get ready for 'salah' (prayer), this young boy in Peshawar, Pakistan, spreads extra prayer mats in the courtyard of the mosque.

Muslims believe that, without Allah's guidance, human beings are not fully able to understand the meaning and purpose of life. They believe that, from the beginning of creation, over a long period of time, Allah sent messengers to earth, to help people to worship the one true God and to show them how to follow a 'straight path' in their behaviour. The first of these messengers, or Prophets, was Adam ﵊. The final messenger was the Prophet Muhammad ﷺ, who lived in Arabia in the sixth to seventh centuries CE (Common Era; see page 47).

Muslims believe that Allah's message was revealed to Muhammad ﷺ, in Arabic, by the angel Jibril (Gabriel). It was Allah's final guidance for people everywhere and at all times. Allah's own words were spoken to Muhammad ﷺ, and these were written down to form the Qur'an, which is the Muslim holy book. The Qur'an must never be changed. Muslims around the world learn to recite the Qur'an in Arabic, whatever their mother tongue.

It is written in the Qur'an:

> Allah invites to the abode of peace, and leads whom He wills to a straight path. (Qur'an 10: 25)

This means that anyone can choose Islam as his or her faith, at any stage of his or her life. There are Muslims of all races and nationalities and from greatly diverse backgrounds. They are all united by their belief in the Shahadah and by certain basic practices which Muslims everywhere must follow. The world-wide community of Muslims is called the 'Ummah'.

Muslim young people on their way home from school, in Sarawak, Malaysia.

A mosque in Mostar, Bosnia, now destroyed in the fighting. Millions of Muslims live in former Yugoslavia.

S L M

The Arabic language is based on root words made up of consonants. For example, the consonants S L M form the root which means 'peace'.

The terms 'Islam', 'Muslim' and 'Salaam' come from that root.

Islam is the state of peaceful obedience to Allah's guidance.

A **Muslim** is someone who believes in and accepts Allah's commands and is at peace with himself or herself and with everything in creation.

As-salamu alaykum (Peace be upon you) are the words Muslims say when they meet.

The Shahadah, written above the entrance to a mosque in Istanbul, Turkey.

Muslims must follow these practices. They help them to be more aware of Allah in everything they do.

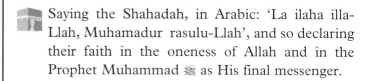

Saying the Shahadah, in Arabic: 'La ilaha illa-Llah, Muhamadur rasulu-Llah', and so declaring their faith in the oneness of Allah and in the Prophet Muhammad ﷺ as His final messenger.

Communicating with and worshipping Allah five times each day, in the way that Muhammad ﷺ taught. This is called 'salah'. Prayers are recited in Arabic.

Fasting from before dawn until sunset every day during the Islamic month of Ramadan. This fasting is called 'sawm'.

Paying an annual welfare due of 2.5% of what wealth remains after personal and business expenditure. This is called 'zakah'.

At least once in one's lifetime, going on pilgrimage to Makkah, Mina, Muzdalifah and Arafat, from the 8th to the 13th of the Islamic month of Dhul Hijjah. This pilgrimage is called 'Hajj'.

Muslims believe that this life is temporary; that it is a trial, in preparation for 'Akhirah', the hereafter. On the Day of Judgement, they will be asked to account for their actions in this life, which the angels have recorded. Therefore Muslims try to lead purposeful and active lives, although they believe that Allah has the final control over what will happen to them.

1

THE STORY OF ISLAM

Allah's messengers

Muslims trace the roots of Islam to Adam ﷺ, the first man. They believe that he was the first of a large number of Prophets. For Muslims, Prophets were people sent by Allah to teach humankind how to behave towards all that He had created and how to worship Him as the one true God.

The Prophet Ibrahim ﷺ lived 4,000 years ago in the Middle East. He showed people that it was useless and wrong to worship idols. It is written in the Qur'an that Ibrahim ﷺ and his son, Isma'il ﷺ, built 'Bayt Allah' (the House of Allah) in Makkah and invited everyone to worship there. Another name for this building is the 'Ka'bah', which means 'cube-shaped'.

Twenty-five of the Prophets sent by Allah to humankind are mentioned in the Qur'an. Many of them are also found in the Torah and the Bible (the books of the Jewish and the Christian religions). Some of them are Ibrahim ﷺ (Abraham), Isma'il ﷺ (Ishmael), Musa ﷺ (Moses), Dawud ﷺ (David) and Isa ﷺ (Jesus).

Today the Ka'bah is within the grand mosque in Makkah. The mosque has been extended many times, to make room for the growing numbers of pilgrims.

IBRAHIM TEACHES AGAINST IDOL WORSHIP

'Behold,' he said to his father and his people. 'What are these images to which you are so devoted?'

They said, 'We found our fathers worshipping them.'

He said, 'Indeed you have been in plain error - you and your fathers... and by Allah, I will certainly plan against your idols ...'

So he broke them to pieces, all but the biggest of them...

They said, 'Who has done this to our gods? ... Are you the one that did this with our gods, O Ibrahim?'

He said, 'No. This was done by this biggest one! Ask them, if they can talk.' ...

Then they were confounded with shame; they said, 'You know full well these idols do not speak!'

Ibrahim said, 'Do you then worship, beside Allah, things which can neither be of any good to you nor do you harm?... Have you no sense?'
(Qur'an 21: 52-67)

Muslims believe that, as time went by, Ibrahim's teachings were forgotten. Allah sent more Prophets, but always people eventually ignored some of their teachings or changed them to suit themselves.

The Prophet Muhammad ﷺ

Muslims believe that the Prophet Muhammad ﷺ is the final Prophet. He was born in the city of Makkah in 570 CE. At this time people had forgotten the one true God. They had filled the Ka'bah with idols and were making money from pilgrims who came there.

Muhammad ﷺ used to go away from the bustle of the city to spend time quietly alone, contemplating, in a desert cave. One night while he was there he suddenly heard the angel Jibril instruct him to 'Proclaim'.

Proclaim, in the name of your Lord and Cherisher, who created man from a clot of blood. Proclaim and your Lord is Most Bountiful - He who taught the use of the pen taught man that which he knew not. (Qur'an 96: 1-5)

At first he was afraid, but when the angel had said the same words three times, he realized that he should repeat and learn what he was being told. This revelation introduced Muhammad ﷺ to his new way of life as a Prophet of Allah. For the next twenty-three years he continued to receive the revelations which contain Allah's guidance (the Qur'an) and to proclaim Allah's final message.

The Dome of the Rock in Jerusalem encloses the rock from which Muhammad ﷺ ascended into the heavens on Laylat ul-Miraj. It is a place of pilgrimage for Muslims.

'Laylat ul-Miraj', the 'Night Journey' of the Prophet Muhammad ﷺ, is a miraculous event which affects the daily life of Muslims to this day. On this night the Prophet ﷺ was taken by the angel Jibril from the mosque in Makkah to Mount Moriah in Jerusalem. Here he led all the Prophets in prayer. Then he

LAYLAT UL-QADR

Muhammad ﷺ received the first revelation of the Qur'an on one of the last ten nights of the month of Ramadan. Muslims commemorate it most often on the 27th night of Ramadan. They call it 'Laylat ul-Qadr', the 'Night of Power'.

'The Night of Power is better than 1,000 months. Therein come down the Angels and the Spirit by Allah's permission on every errand: Peace! ... this until the rise of morn!' (Qur'an 97: 3-5)

travelled up through the heavens until he reached the very throne of the Creator. Allah in his mercy revealed to him the order for five obligatory times of prayer (salah) every day and night.

Madinah and its Islamic laws

Many people in Makkah were angry when Muhammad ﷺ told them to behave fairly and not to worship idols. They persecuted him and planned to kill him.

Some people in Yathrib, to the north of Makkah, asked Muhammad ﷺ to become their leader, to settle rivalries between tribes which were upsetting their community. Muhammad ﷺ moved to Yathrib in 622 CE and it became known as 'Madinat-un-Nabi' (City of the Prophet), or Madinah.

Muslims must pray five times a day. At each of these times, all Muslims thank Allah for His mercy as they journey to the Almighty.

To stop the fighting between tribes, Muhammad ﷺ drew up laws, to make sure that everyone was treated fairly and equally. These laws were

The Prophet's Mosque in Madinah has been extended many times to allow more Muslims to offer salah inside.

revolutionary because, until this time, people had been loyal only to their own tribe or family. News soon spread of how the laws worked to help people and, before the Prophet Muhammad ﷺ died in 632 CE, the city of Makkah and many other places in Arabia had accepted to be ruled by Islamic laws.

Sunni and Shi'ah

After the death of Muhammad ﷺ his companion Abu Bakr was chosen by some to lead the community. Others believed that the Prophet ﷺ had wanted Ali ؏, his cousin and son-in-law, to be his successor. Those who felt this became known as the Shi'at Ali (Party of Ali), or Shi'ah for short. The rest became known as Ahl-as-Sunnah wa-l-Ijma (the people of the custom of the Prophet and the consensus) - Sunni for short.

Abu Bakr was succeeded as Khalifah, to lead the community, by Umar, then Uthman and eventually Ali ؏. The death of Ali ؏ in 661 ended the line of 'rightly guided' successors and the division between Sunni and Shi'ah became more marked. Sunni Muslims did not believe that the khalifate should pass only to the family of the Prophet ﷺ or be hereditary. They wanted to be able to elect their leaders. The Shi'ah felt that the sons of Ali ؏ and grandsons of Muhammad ﷺ, Hassan and Hussein ؏, had inherited the spiritual and political leadership of the community.

Yazid, a later Khalifah, demanded the loyalty of Hussein ؏, but Hussein ؏ would not accept him. In 680 Yazid sent an army of 4,000 men to fight against Hussein ؏, who was travelling with his family and supporters. They were massacred, but two of his sons survived and the Shi'ah system of spiritual leadership, known as the Imamate, passed on through them. Most Shi'ah Muslims believe that there have been twelve infallible Imams and that the last of these did not die but will come back to restore justice on earth.

When Sunni Muslim societies have wanted to live entirely by Islamic law, they have tried to bring back the system of the Khalifah, to lead the community.

LAWS FOR MADINAH

Every person must be treated equally. No matter how rich or important their family, all people would have the same justice.

If people were poor or in need they would be helped by money collected from taxes.

The Jewish people in Madinah were free to practise their religion without interference.

If anyone attacked Madinah, all of its citizens would join together to defend one another.

Many Muslims believe that what is needed today is strong religious and political leadership from a good and scholarly Khalifah.

Both Shi'ah and Sunni Muslims, to this day, use the same Qur'an, follow the example of the Prophet ﷺ and share Islamic beliefs.

The spread of Islam

In the hundred years after the death of the Prophet Muhammad ﷺ, Islam spread as far as north Africa and central Asia. These areas had been occupied and ruled by the Roman, Byzantine and Persian Empires, which were unpopular because of their warring and heavy taxes. The people did not resist the Muslim conquerors and even supported them against their previous rulers.

The golden gates to the mosque of Imam Hussein ﷺ, in Kerbala, Iraq. Imam Hussein ﷺ was martyred here in 680 by the armies of Yazid. In the twentieth century, this important place of Shi'ah pilgrimage has been devastated by the armies of Sadam Hussein, president of Iraq.

When the Christian city of Damascus in Syria surrendered to the Muslim leader Khalid ibn Walid in 635 CE, its Bishop brought Khalid food. Khalid promised the inhabitants 'security for their lives, properties and churches... So long as they pay a fair tax, nothing but good shall befall them.' In such ways, Islamic leaders tried to show a good example of Qur'anic teaching.

By the ninth and tenth centuries, Baghdad was the greatest city in the expanding Islamic world. Through contact with China, people here had learned the art of paper-making. This encouraged the production of books, and knowledge of Islam spread.

Islam became established in India in 711 CE, as a result of trading links. By the sixteenth century India was ruled by the Mughal Empire. As most people in India were Hindus, one of the Muslim emperors, Akbar, made a Hindu his second in command. He also ordered Muslims not to kill cows, which Hindus consider sacred.

KEY DATES IN THE HISTORY OF ISLAM

BEFORE THE COMMON ERA

In the beginning   The Prophet Adam ﷺ is created.

2000   The Prophets Ibrahim ﷺ and Isma'il ﷺ build the Ka'bah in Makkah.

1200   The Prophet Musa ﷺ is given the Taurat (Torah) by Allah.

1000   The Prophet Dawud ﷺ is given the Zabur (Book of Psalms) by Allah.

COMMON ERA

1st century   The Prophet Isa ﷺ is born.

570   The Prophet Muhammad ﷺ is born in Makkah in Arabia.

610   The Prophet Muhammad ﷺ receives the first revelation of the Qur'an.

622   The Prophet Muhammad ﷺ migrates to Madinah and establishes the first Islamic state. This is counted as the beginning (year 1) of the Islamic calendar.

632   The Prophet Muhammad ﷺ dies in Madinah.

632 - 661   The period of the Khalifahs. After the death of the Prophet ﷺ Abu Bakr became the first Khalifah (successor), to lead the community. In Sunni tradition he is followed by Umar, Uthman and Ali (May Allah be pleased with them).

632 - early 10th century   The period of the Imams. In Shi'ah tradition, spiritual and political leadership of the community passed from the Prophet ﷺ to the twelve Imams, through his cousin Ali ﷺ.

680   The martyrdom of Imam Hussein ﷺ at Kerbala, Iraq.

711   Muslims enter Spain and begin Islamic rule.

750 – 850   The Shari'ah (the Islamic system of law) is developed.

970   The Islamic University of al-Azhar is founded in Cairo, Egypt. It is the world's oldest university.

1138 - 93   Lifetime of Salah ud-Din, Governor of Egypt, adversary of Richard the Lion Heart and victor in the Crusades. Salah ud-Din is a model of Islamic chivalrous behaviour.

c.1300   Osman, who gives his name to the Ottoman dynasty, begins to establish his power in Turkey.

KEY DATES IN THE HISTORY OF ISLAM

1453	The Ottomans conquer Constantinople, capital of the Byzantine Empire, and rename it Istanbul. The Ottoman Empire expands and by the 1520s it includes south-east Europe (including most of Hungary), the Middle East and north Africa.
1492	Muslim rule in Spain ends.
1550	A Muslim kingdom is established in Sumatra. From here, Islam spreads to Java, the Moluccas and Borneo. In the seventeenth century there is a 'golden age' of Islam in Indonesia.
1798	Egypt, under Muslim rule since 672, is occupied by France.
1809	Usman dan Fodio founds the Khalifate of Sokoto in Nigeria.
1827	Britain, France and Russia support Greece against its Ottoman rulers.
1830	The French invade Algeria.
1873	The Dutch attack the Sumatran Muslim kingdom.
1882	The British attack and occupy Alexandria, Egypt.
1894	Britain's first purpose-built mosque is completed in Woking, Surrey.
1915	The Constantinople agreement between Britain, France and Russia on the division of Ottoman lands.
1917	The British fight the Ottomans for control of Gaza in Palestine.
1922	The end of the Ottoman Empire and Khalifate.
1927	The Persian Shah abolishes Islamic dress and rules that all men must wear European-style clothes and hats.
1954	The Algerians rebel against French colonial rule.
1950s - 60s	Muslims migrate to Europe, the USA, Australia and throughout Arabia.
1979	The Persian Shah is deposed and the Islamic Republic of Iran is established.
1990s	Genocide of Muslims in Bosnia, Burma and Chechnya.

ISLAM IN SPAIN

In 711 CE a Muslim army of North African Berbers (a nomadic people) landed in Spain and gained control of a large part of the country. Europeans called them the Moors.

In the tenth to the eleventh centuries, Córdoba, the capital of Muslim Spain, became the most splendid city in Europe. There was street lighting, many homes had running water and there were hundreds of public baths. Very few people in Europe at this time could read or write, but in Muslim Spain there was primary education for all and so nearly everyone became literate. Most of the education was based in the 700 mosques in Córdoba and lectures were given there. Advances were made in medicine, science, astronomy, music and the classification of libraries. Scholars from other parts of Europe came to study under great masters such as ibn Rushd and ibn al-Arabi.

Inside the Great Mosque in Córdoba, famed for its beautiful arches.

From India, Islam spread through Muslim missionaries and traders to south-east Asia, Malaysia, Indonesia and the Philippines. One attraction of Islam was its followers' belief in the equality of all people. This was also a reason for the spread of Islam to the west African countries of Mali, Senegal, Nigeria and Ghana between the eighth and the eighteenth centuries.

Because Islam encourages its followers to learn about Allah's creation, cities under Muslim rule became centres of learning. Timbuktu in Mali grew up around its mosque. Its students opened Qur'an schools throughout west Africa, which continue teaching Islamic studies today.

THE OTTOMAN EMPIRE

When the Ottomans captured Constantinople in 1453, their leader, Sultan Mehmet II, renamed the city Istanbul. To help it develop, he invited Muslims and Jews who were suffering persecution in Spain and other parts of Europe to make their homes there. In 1560 the Sulmaniyyah mosque complex was completed, including the mosque, seven colleges, a hospital, an asylum, a soup kitchen, a bath-house, schools, shops, a sports ground and fountains.

The Empire expanded to rule much of the Islamic world. Everywhere, roads and rest houses for travellers were built, and there was an efficient system of legal and social services.

However, at the beginning of the nineteenth century the Empire came under pressure. Austria and Russia took much of its northern territories and France, Britain and Russia made a treaty to help Greece against the Ottomans. In 1918, at the end of the First World War, France, Britain, Russia, Holland and Italy ruled nearly all of the countries of north-west and east Africa, the Middle East, India, south-east and central Asia.

Europe and the Islamic world

The European colonial powers imposed their own legal and social systems on their colonies, in place of the existing Islamic ones. Many Muslims in the colonies were taught that European systems were better than those of Islam, about which they were able to learn very little.

Since the colonies gained their independence in the latter part of the twentieth century, Muslims there have been trying to re-establish the teachings and institutions of Islam.

As a result of the connections made between Europe and the Islamic world, many Muslims have settled in Europe. There are also increasing numbers of converts to Islam, and so Muslims today make up the second largest religious group in Europe. They are maintaining the teachings and practices of Islam, building mosques and joining in activities and work which can benefit the whole community.

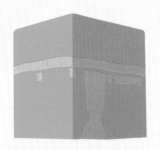

2

THE WORLD OF ISLAM

There are large numbers of Muslims world-wide, as the map on pages 20-21 shows. Wherever Islam becomes established, it accepts cultural customs which are not in conflict with Islamic teaching.

This chapter looks at the experience of Muslims in three very different parts of the world: Iran, the USA and central Asia.

Iran

Iran is a huge country, bigger than Britain, France, Germany and Italy together. Ninety-eight per cent of the population are Muslims, most of whom are Shi'ahs.

In 1979 Shi'ah Muslims established the Islamic Republic of Iran. Its leader is a Shi'ah 'ayatollah' (sign of Allah) - that is, someone who has studied Islamic theology and law, to a very high degree, at one of the famous religious colleges in Tabriz, Qumm or Mashad.

These colleges take students from all over the world. They may progress from being a 'mullah' (scholar) to 'hujjat-ul-Islam' (proof of Islam), and at that stage they may be invited by existing ayatollahs to join their ranks. The ayatollahs are greatly respected for their knowledge and ability to make religious and legal decisions.

The huge scale and beautiful craftsmanship of this mosque in Isfahan reflect the Islamic understanding of the power and magnificence of Allah Almighty.

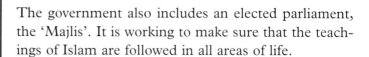

A mullah in a mosque at Isfahan. Spending time in quiet prayer and concentration is part of his spiritual training before he is able to teach others.

The government also includes an elected parliament, the 'Majlis'. It is working to make sure that the teachings of Islam are followed in all areas of life.

Beautiful mosques were built in Isfahan and other cities in the land of Iran, during its 'golden age' of Islam in the seventeenth century. The books of some of the most famous poets and mystics of Islam are kept in the library of rare books and ancient Qur'ans in Mashad.

African American Muslims

Most African Americans in the USA today are descendants of more than 10 million west African Muslims who were taken as slaves to America in the seventeenth and eighteenth centuries. The slave masters disregarded the Africans' own religion and culture, and taught them Christianity.

Only fifty years after slavery was abolished, African Americans became interested in Islam. In 1914, Noble Ali Drew gave his followers Muslim names and taught them about the Prophet Muhammad ﷺ. He gave them identity cards which said they were 'Moorish Americans', in memory of the north Africans who had conquered Spain for Islam in the eighth century. He wanted them to shake off the identity forced on them by slavery.

In 1930, a man called Wallace Fard appeared in the poor areas of Detroit, saying that he had come from Makkah and that African Americans were the 'lost-found tribe of Shabazz'. He named Elijah Muhammad to follow him as their next leader and, over the next thirty years, the Honourable Elijah Muhammad and growing numbers of followers set up schools, universities and 'temples of Islam'. This new 'Nation of Islam' helped start many black-run businesses and encouraged women and girls to train for jobs. People were taught to stay away from alcohol, drugs and smoking, to have self-respect, and not to trust white people.

In the 1960s, a man named Malcolm X became the spokesperson for the Nation of Islam. He became well-known in the civil rights movement, and white Americans grew fearful of the influence and power of the 'Black Muslims'.

Malcolm X left the Nation of Islam and in 1964 made the Hajj (pilgrimage) to Makkah. This gave him a new understanding of Islam and, on his return to the USA, now named Al Hajj Malik al Shabbaz, he began to teach that Islam gives equality to all, black and white.

Today, crowds of African American Muslims gather for Id prayer in a Washington park.

> America needs to understand Islam, because this is the one religion that erases from its society the race problem. Throughout my travels in the Muslim world... I have... seen sincere and true brotherhood practised by all colours together...

Such words made many people uneasy and Malcolm X was assassinated. However, his ideas took root. By the 1980s, most of the 2 million African American Muslims followed the same teachings and practices of Islam as Muslims world-wide.

The clothing Muslim men wear when they go on Hajj (see page 40) makes them all look alike. Seeing everyone like this, without status symbols or titles, is a powerful reminder that all are equal before Allah.

MUSLIMS AROUND THE WORLD

There are Muslims living in almost every country on earth, totalling more than one thousand million.

CANADA
0.25 million

USA
6 million

Austria	150,000
Belgium	450,000
Eire	9,000
Greece	200,000
Holland	500,000
Italy	100,000
Portugal	20,000
Switzerland	155,000
Yugoslavia (former)	6,000,000

BRAZIL
0.25 million

ARGENTINA
0.5 million

It is estimated that one out of every five people in the world is a Muslim, and one out of every eight women is a Muslim.

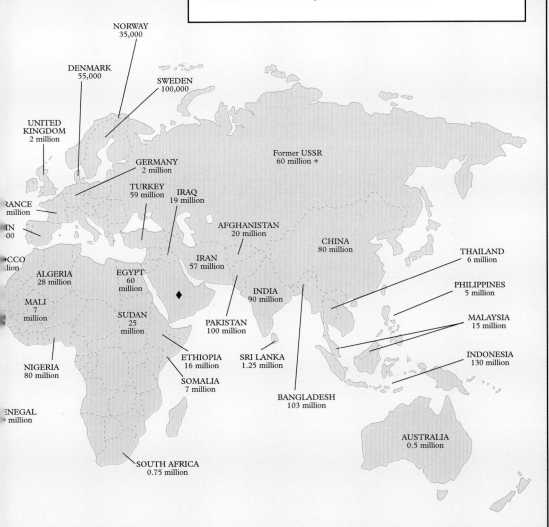

♦ More than 130 million predominantly Muslim Arabic-speaking people live in 20 Middle Eastern and Gulf States, not including several million Muslims living in the occupied territories of Palestine, West Bank and Gaza.

NORWAY
35,000

DENMARK
55,000

SWEDEN
100,000

UNITED
KINGDOM
2 million

GERMANY
2 million

Former USSR
60 million +

TURKEY
59 million

IRAQ
19 million

RANCE
million

AFGHANISTAN
20 million

CHINA
80 million

THAILAND
6 million

IN
00

IRAN
57 million

CCO
lion

ALGERIA
28 million

EGYPT
60
million

INDIA
90 million

PHILIPPINES
5 million

MALI
7
million

MALAYSIA
15 million

SUDAN
25
million

PAKISTAN
100 million

INDONESIA
130 million

NIGERIA
80 million

ETHIOPIA
16 million

SRI LANKA
1.25 million

SOMALIA
7 million

BANGLADESH
103 million

ENEGAL
million

AUSTRALIA
0.5 million

SOUTH AFRICA
0.75 million

There are 46 Muslim majority states in Asia and Africa.

Trade from the eastern Mediterranean to China helped spread Islam all along the Silk Route. Samarkand, in the heart of central Asia, developed as a remarkable and beautiful city.

In the fifteenth century its ruler, Ulugh Beg built a huge observatory and wrote an encyclopedia about the courses and positions of stars. Land travellers across the central Asian deserts, like sailors, needed to navigate by the stars. It was also important for travelling Muslims to be able to work out the direction of qibla (see page 32) and the start of the lunar months.

Built in 1807, the 'Char Minar' in Bukhara was the gatehouse to a madrasah funded by a wealthy merchant.

Islamic revival in central Asia

Fifty million Muslims live in five central Asian republics: Uzbekistan, Kazakhstan, Tajikistan, Kirgizia and Turkmenia. These republics became self-governing in the early 1990s, after seventy years of Communist rule as part of the USSR.

From the late 1920s, people had been forbidden to practise and teach their faith. Many Muslims continued to learn the Qur'an and about Islam, in secret. However, the mosques fell into disuse.

Before Communist rule, the city of Bukhara had 360 mosques. Now the people there are restoring the 120 mosques and madrasahs (Islamic schools and colleges) that are left, turning them from empty monuments back to busy places of worship and learning.

During Communist rule, only small official groups were allowed to go on Hajj. 'Now,' says Jamila Nishan from Ashkabad in Turkmenia, 'lots of central Asian Muslims will be able to visit the holy places of Islam and meet Muslims from all over the world.'

3

SOURCES OF ISLAM

The Qur'an

Muslims sometimes call the Qur'an 'our maker's handbook'. They believe that the words in it are Allah's own words, exactly as they were revealed to the Prophet Muhammad ﷺ. They also believe that the revelations made to Muhammad ﷺ were and are Allah's final guidance for people everywhere. The word 'Qur'an' means 'that which should be read'.

With their Qur'ans carefully wrapped, these girls in India are off to learn how to read and pronounce the Arabic words of Allah's revealed book.

Allah's message was revealed to Muhammad ﷺ by the angel Jibril in Arabic at different times and in different places over a period of twenty-three years. Each year, during the month of Ramadan, Muhammad ﷺ recited what he had been taught, to make sure that he had memorized it correctly. By the time of his death, all the revelations had been written down to form the Qur'an. Many Muslim men and women knew the whole Qur'an by heart.

HAFIZ

There are millions of people today who know the whole Qur'an by heart. They are called 'Hafiz'. The beautiful rhythmic language of the Qur'an and the sense of the words make it easy to memorize.

All Muslims learn to recite at least some short 'surahs' (sections), such as 'Al-Fatihah' and 'Al-Iklaas', in Arabic so that they can perform their salah in the correct way. But often people read and study the Qur'an in their own mother tongue. There are translations into many languages.

How the Qur'an is arranged

The Qur'an is arranged in 114 surahs, and each surah consists of a number of 'ayat' ('signs').

The whole of the text is divided into thirty equal parts, for people who wish to read the complete Qur'an in daily sections over one month. It is also divided into seven equal parts, for people who want to read the whole Qur'an in one week.

Using the Qur'an

The Qur'an is recited by Muslims on almost every occasion in life, for example when remembering someone who has died or when giving thanks for success or a happy event. Many Muslims try to read a section of Qur'an every day. Lots of people have a pocket-sized copy with a zipped plastic cover which they take everywhere and can read, for example, on the bus or the train.

Where books are expensive, as in Gambia, classes learn to read the surahs from wooden boards, which are strong and last a long time.

AL-FATIHAH

'Al-Fatihah' ('The Opener') is surah 1 of the Qur'an. Muslims recite it at least seventeen times each day, during the five times of salah. It is also usually the first part of the Qur'an that Muslim children learn. Muslims think of it as the essence of the Qur'an and the Perfect Prayer, through which they offer worship and ask for guidance. It sums up their relationship with Allah.

> In the name of Allah, Most Gracious, Most Merciful.
> Praise be to Allah, Lord of the Worlds,
> The Most Gracious, the Most Merciful;
> Master of the Day of Judgement.
> You alone we worship and You alone we ask for help.
> Guide us on the straight way, the way of those You have favoured,
> Not the path of those who earn Your anger, nor of those who go astray.

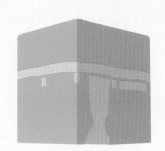

AL-IKLAAS

'Al-Iklaas' (which means 'sincerity' or 'purity of faith') is surah 112. It announces the most important idea in Islam, which is 'tawhid' - the oneness of Allah. This surah says that polytheism, believing in lots of gods, is wrong and also that people should not try to picture Allah as a human being. This is usually the second part of the Qur'an that Muslim children are taught.

In the name of Allah, Most Gracious, Most
  Merciful.
Say: He is Allah the One.
Allah, the Eternal and Absolute
He begets not, nor is he begotten.
And there is none like Him.

Hadith

The Hadith are reports of the sayings and actions of the Prophet Muhammad ﷺ, collected in the first century after his death. Each hadith comes with information about when the Prophet ﷺ said the words, or did what he did, and who heard or saw it. For example, Anas ibn Malik, who was employed by the Prophet ﷺ as a servant, reported that the Prophet ﷺ said:

None of you truly believes until you wish for others what you wish for yourself. (al-Bukhari and Muslim)

The Ka'bah (see page 7) has a beautiful cover embroidered in gold thread with words from the Qur'an.

Many scholars spent their lives making sure that everything written about the sayings and actions of the Prophet ﷺ was true. They checked the honesty of everyone who gave a report. They considered whether the

THE SUNNAH

All the customs and examples of the Prophet Muhammad's ﷺ behaviour, reports of what he said and did and stories about his life are called the Sunnah. The Hadith and Sirah (the Prophet's ﷺ biography) are included in and considered part of the Sunnah.

The Sunnah is not in book form, like the collections of hadith and the biography. It is the totality of everything known about the Prophet ﷺ. Together they are a source of guidance for Muslims about what to do and how to behave.

statement or action was reasonable, whether it matched the way the Prophet ﷺ spoke, and whether it was in accordance with the teaching of the Qur'an. If they were satisfied, they accepted the report for their collection of hadith. Many thousands of hadith were agreed as true. Some of the most famous collections are Biharul Anwar, al-Bukhari, al Kafi and Muslim.

Two other hadith are:

> Part of someone's being a good Muslim is leaving alone that which does not concern them. (Tirmidhi)

> If a believer plants a tree, or sows a field, and people and beasts and birds eat from it, all of it is charity on his/her part. (Muslim)

Shari'ah - Islamic law

In the eighth century, ways of understanding and interpreting the Qur'an and Sunnah were developed by scholars who founded the main schools of Islamic law. The Arabic word 'Shari'ah' means 'a path to be followed'.

Muslims believe that Allah is the ruler and judge of everything and everyone, and that human beings have the duty to look after everything Allah has created. The Muslim community uses Islamic law to try to uphold these beliefs. For example, the Shari'ah does not allow anyone to exploit natural resources such as water, oil or coal for their own selfish advantage.

Islamic law is able to deal with new developments, for instance in science, in a positive way. This is done by examining the Qur'an and Sunnah, applying reason, consulting knowledgeable people and taking account of public interest. When the question of test-tube babies was considered in this way, the conclusion was that, as long as the egg to be fertilized and the sperm used were from the husband and wife of a married couple, the process was acceptable. It would not be acceptable to use either donor eggs or donor sperm.

4
HOME AND FAMILY LIFE

Muslims believe that the home should be a place of comfort where everyone can live, eat and pray in an Islamic way.

It is Allah Who made your dwellings homes of rest and quiet for you. (Qur'an 16: 80)

Calling the adhan from a mosque in Cairo, Egypt.

Prayer

The five times of prayer, or salah, are worked out by the position of the sun, so they vary from day to day through the year. In Islamic countries, the 'adhan' (call to prayer) is made from the mosque to let everyone know that it is prayer time.

Muslim families in all countries usually offer their early morning and night-time prayers together at home, and this helps everyone to learn and keep up their salah. Muslim homes have prayer mats and a space to pray. To keep the home, and especially the

PRAYER TIMES IN BRITAIN

Salat-ul-Fajr is prayed between the first light of dawn and sunrise. In winter in Britain this can be as late as 6.43 am and in summer as early as 2.39 am.

Salat-ul-Zuhr is prayed after midday. This varies between 11.50 am in winter and 1.13 pm in summer.

Salat-ul-Asr is the mid-afternoon prayer: as early as 2 pm in winter and as late as 5.19 pm in summer.

Salat-ul-Maghrib is the sunset prayer: as early as 3.51 pm in winter, and after 9 pm in summer.

Salat-ul-Isha is prayed from about an hour and a half after Maghrib.

27

Washing before salah.

prayer place, clean, many families leave their outdoor shoes at the front door.

Before salah, everyone washes in a special way called 'wudu'. This means washing hands, mouth, nose, face, arms, head, ears, neck and feet three times each in running water. Some people splash a lot and make the floor wet!

AN ISLAMIC HOME IN CYPRUS

Eleven-year-old Habiba Mustafa lives with her family in a traditional old Islamic-style house in northern Cyprus. The house is built around a beautiful flower-filled courtyard garden, watered from a central fountain. To the left and right of the main door are separate guest sitting rooms for men and for women. All the family's bedrooms, kitchen and sitting rooms are on the far side of the courtyard. There is also a 'hamam' or Turkish bathhouse with a domed roof. The water tank for the hamam is heated by a fire.

Because Habiba's father is a scholar who teaches about Islam, many students come to visit and listen to his talks about the Qur'an and the Sunnah. Two large adjoining prayer rooms on the third side of the courtyard are used by the family and visitors for these occasions and when it is time for salah.

Even though their house is old-fashioned and made of mud bricks and wood, Habiba's mother likes it far better than her sister's modern flat. 'Our house is cool in the summer, warm in the winter, and is pleasant to live in,' she says.

Mealtimes

At the beginning of a meal in a Muslim home, everyone says the words 'Bismillah-ir Rahman-ir-Rahim', which mean 'In the name of Allah All Gracious All Merciful'.

As in all areas of their lives, Muslims try to follow the example of the Prophet Muhammad ﷺ at mealtimes. It is part of the Sunnah to offer food to guests and to share food made for family and religious celebrations with neighbours. If all the food, such as rice or couscous together with meat or vegetables, is served on one large plate, then it is 'good manners' for each person to eat only from the part nearest to him or her, using the right hand.

Food prepared for a feast in Kashmir. 'So, eat of the sustenance Allah has provided for you, lawful and good; and be grateful for the favours of Allah' (Qur'an 16: 114).

No matter how lovely it is, Muslims are taught not to rush their food and not to be greedy, and to make sure that everyone at the table has enough to eat. The Prophet Muhammad ﷺ said that it was best for the stomach to be one-third full, one-third with water, and one-third empty.

In Morocco, after a meal, a pitcher of water, a basin and a hand towel are brought so that everyone can rinse their hands.

Food

What we eat and drink affects our bodies and health. Islam teaches that some things are good, while others are harmful. Food and drink which Muslims are allowed to eat is called 'halal', which means 'permitted'. There are recipes for Muslim dishes from all over the world, but even beefburgers and sausages are halal, provided that they are made with halal ingredients.

THE RAMADAN FAST

During Ramadan, Muslims eat and drink nothing during the hours of daylight. They have a pre-dawn meal called 'Sahoor' and a meal called 'Iftar' to break the fast at sunset. Families prepare especially nourishing meals for Sahoor. For Iftar, people in north Africa have a thick soup called 'harira'. The fast is broken in Arabia with dates and Arabic coffee; in Turkey, with olives and tea; and in India, with sweet milky drinks and fruit.

Fasting reminds Muslims of how dependent people are on food to give them energy. Most of all it makes them aware of and grateful to Allah, who provides all food.

Muslims may eat:

meat from any sheep, chicken, goat or cow which has been killed by a butcher who says 'Bismillah Allahu Akbar' ('In the name of Allah, Allah is Most Great'); any edible vegetable or fruit; the eggs of halal birds.

Muslims may not eat or drink any of the following, which are 'haram' (forbidden):

the meat of pigs, including bacon, ham, pork or any product made from pig; the meat of any animal, bird or other creature which has died naturally, or which has been strangled; any reptiles, birds or animals which are carnivorous; any kind of alcohol. Food containing alcohol is also forbidden.

Some Muslims also do not eat shellfish.

HOME IN THE USA

When Zeba Sadiq's family moved from Palestine to Colorado in the USA, they were the only Muslims in the area. There was nowhere to buy halal food, and so they bought from the kosher grocery store. Zeba's mother bought meat, stock cubes, biscuits and other things there, because she could be sure they would be free from any pork.

As the Muslim community in Colorado grew, shops opened to serve their needs. Now the Muslims have arrangements with local farmers to provide them with meat prepared under halal conditions.

One of Zeba's favourite meals is Bukhari rice. The recipe has been in her family for generations and is made with rice, meat and home-grown carrots. Zeba is a keen gardener and thinks that Colorado carrots are the sweetest.

The roles of family members

Older family members follow the teachings and practices of Islam in all they do, so that children can learn from their example. There is an Arab saying that 'The mother is a school'. Children are taught modest behaviour, self-respect and respect for others, good manners, honesty and consideration. They often learn to be charitable by sharing food with neighbours and people in need.

Fathers also have an important role. They must provide for their family to the best of their ability. Within his home, a father is the 'Imam' for his family.

With his sisters and little brother behind him, this young 'Imam' is practising leading his family in salah.

An understanding of responsibilities within the family is taken from the Qur'an and the Sunnah. Here are some examples:

> The right due to the child from its parents is for them to teach it writing, swimming and archery ... and provide it with nothing but what is wholesome. (Hadith al-Bukhari)

> A man was sitting with the Prophet when his son came in. The man kissed him and sat him on his lap. Then his daughter came in and he let her sit down in front of him. The Prophet said: 'Shouldn't you have treated them the same?' (The Sirah)

> ... be kind to parents whether one or both of them reach old age in your life. Never speak badly to them but always speak to them with respect. And out of kindness, lower over them the wing of tenderness and say, 'Oh my Lord, Have mercy on them as they cared for me when I was a child.' (Qur'an 17:23)

5

COMMUNITY LIFE

The Ka'bah in Makkah is the first house dedicated to the worship of Allah. To perform their salah, as Allah has ordered, Muslims world-wide turn in the direction of Makkah. In Britain this means facing south-east.

This mosque in Brunei has lots of room for women to perform salah. It was built in 1958, to the order of the Sultan at that time.

The mosque

Mosques can look very different, from the outside. In west Africa they may be made from mud, and in China and Indonesia, from carved wood. In Iran and Turkey mosques are often covered in beautifully coloured tiles. In Arabia many mosques are simply painted white. But, inside, all mosques have:

a 'mihrab', an alcove in one wall, which shows the direction to face for prayer. This direction is called 'qibla'.

if large enough, a 'minbar', a platform, where the Imam stands to speak to the people.

a prayer area for men, and often one for women.

Either inside, or near it, every mosque has a place for people to wash, ready for prayer. And many larger mosques have an open courtyard and a minaret, from which the adhan is called. In north Africa the minaret is traditionally a tall, square tower. In Turkey, it is slim and round like a pencil.

Before entering the prayer hall people take off their shoes and either leave them on a rack or put them in a plastic bag to take with them. Inside there is no furniture, as people stand, bow and kneel and sit on their heels to worship. Very old people or those with disabilities may perform their salah sitting on a chair.

Mosques built from mud, like this one in Mali, stay refreshingly cool inside.

The Imam

The work of an Imam is to lead the five daily prayers; to give a talk at the midday Friday prayer; to perform marriages and funerals; to answer people's questions about Islamic teaching and practices; and to give advice to people about their problems. To lead men and women in salah, the Imam must be a man, but a group of all women may choose a woman to lead their salah. Large mosques in towns and cities may have one or more full-time Imams.

Other people at the mosque

Many other people work at important national mosques, including guides to

An intricately tiled and painted mihrab in an old mosque in Bangladesh.

Friday is the day of the week for Muslims to come together to pray the midday prayer and to listen to the 'khutbah', a talk by the Imam about religious, topical and practical matters. Most Muslims in non-Muslim countries are sad if, because of work or school, they or their children miss the Salat ul-Jumu'ah.

This Muslim in Thailand is refreshing and preparing himself by washing before salah.

show visitors around. Some of these mosques have offices, libraries, a bookshop, classrooms for madrasahs, where children and adults are taught the Qur'an, halls for weddings, lectures and community events, and kitchens from which food is provided, especially in Ramadan. One office job is to distribute zakah, the welfare tax which all Muslims who can afford to must pay each year. The mosques also employ someone to prepare dead bodies for burial.

The jammah

Generally, the men, women and children who use the mosque all share the work of running it. This local community is called the 'jammah' and has the following responsibilities:

to meet together once a week for Salat ul-Jumu'ah and khutbah;
to make sure that, when they have sufficient resources, no one among them is struggling in poverty or hardship;
to settle any disputes which occur in the community;
to try to help the community in the areas of Islamic education, health, and social and moral welfare.

The Prophet Muhammad ﷺ said: 'The Muslim community is like a single body. When one part is afflicted the other parts feel pain and fever' (Hadith Muslim).

A jammah can begin with a few Muslims who live or work in the same district, coming together to find a place to hold the Friday prayer. They may use part of someone's home, shop or office for salah and as a madrasah, while they save up for larger accommodation.

AN IMAM IN HOLLAND

Ahmad Patishuwissa is an Imam in Ridderkerk, a small town in Holland. The community he looks after has built a beautiful little mosque to a modern design. The families of many people in his jammah came originally from Indonesia in south-east Asia and Surinam in south America. Because of marriages and large numbers of Dutch people accepting Islam, the jammah is multi-racial.

Ahmad teaches the Qur'an to adults and children on three evenings per week and on Saturday mornings. He also leads the Friday prayer and all the Id celebrations. His family say that his work doesn't stop there. His daughter, Kerima, says: 'People often come to our house to ask my dad's advice and get his help with all kinds of things, from money problems to health worries. If he can't help them himself, he usually knows someone who can.'

The Ummah

Muslims believe that they belong to a world-wide community, called the 'Ummah', or Nation of Muhammad. It is not important that they were born in different countries and have different customs; what matters is that they are all united as one community by their belief in Islam. Muslims are pleased that the Ummah is made up of people of all races, without any distinction between them.

Mankind. We created you from a single pair of a male and a female,
And made you into nations and tribes, that you may know each other.
(Not that you may despise each other.)
(Qur'an 49:13)

Muslim parents prefer to name their children after a good person, or choose names with a good meaning.

Many boys are named after Allah's Prophets: for example, Ibrahim, Idris, Ilyas and Muhammad.

Other popular boys' names refer to the qualities of Allah. An example is Abdul Karim, which means 'slave of the Bountiful'. It would be wrong to call someone 'Abdul' (slave of) on its own. It would also be wrong to call someone just 'Karim', because that is Allah's name.

Girls are often named after women in the family of the Prophet Muhammad ﷺ, such as his daughter, Fatimah Zahrah, and his wife, Khadijah.

6

A MUSLIM LIFETIME

All important events in a Muslim lifetime, such as birth, marriage and death, are marked in a simple way which involves the Muslim community. There is no ceremony or ritual. Social customs surrounding each event may vary from country to country, but the central Islamic practice is the same world-wide.

Birth

The birth of a baby is a happy occasion. Muslims say that a baby is a gift from Allah and brings 'barakah' (blessings). The first words a new-born child should hear are those of the adhan, which are whispered into his or her right ear. The words of the 'iqamah' are spoken into the left ear.

When a baby is about a week old, family and friends are invited to celebrate his or her naming. The adhan and the iqamah are said again, and a taste of honey may be put on the baby's tongue, to link the sweet words with the sweet taste. The baby's hair may be shaved and the tiny amount of hair weighed on some goldsmith's or pharmacist's scales. The family then makes a gift to charity of the value of the same weight of silver.

Circumcision

Following the Sunnah of the Prophet ﷺ, Muslim boys are circumcised. In some cases this happens in the first few days after birth. In Morocco it is more usual to wait until the boy is four or five and, in Turkey, even ten.

Growing up

By joining in the family religious activities, Muslim children learn to pray, to be clean for prayer, to be

THE ADHAN AND THE IQAMAH

The adhan is the Muslim call to prayer. Each line is said twice, except for the last line which is said once:

Allahu Akbar	Allah is most Great!
Allahu Akbar	Allah is most Great!
Ashhadu an la ilaha illa-Llah	I testify there is no god but Allah.
Asshadu anna Muhammad ar-Rasulullah	I testify that Muhammad is the Messenger of Allah.
Hayyi'ala-s-salah	Hasten to prayer!
Hayyi'alal-falah	Hasten to prosperity!
Allahu Akbar	Allah is most Great!
La ilaha illa-llah	There is no god but Allah.

The iqamah is the call to stand up for prayer. It is the same as the adhan except that, after 'Hayyi'alal-falah', these words are added, said twice:

Qad qamat as-salah	Prayer has started.

modest, and to understand the basics of Islam. From an early age they learn to read the Qur'an, at home or at a local madrasah or at a mosque. From when they are seven, their parents must tell them to pray at the five prayer times.

After puberty, young people are responsible themselves for carrying out Islamic practices, including performing salah five times daily and fasting during the whole month of Ramadan. Schools with pupils from a variety of faiths often set aside a room where Muslim pupils can pray at lunchtime and in the late afternoon in winter.

Teachers in these schools are sometimes worried that it is unhealthy for young people to fast. Neither Islam nor Muslim parents are cruel. Young people come to no harm when they

Muslim children in Kashgar, western China.

The hijab is simply a scarf large enough to cover the neck and chest. It is not a face-covering veil. All Muslims must dress modestly, in loose-fitting, non-transparent clothes. They wear styles suitable for their occupation and for the climate and culture of where they live.

fast during Ramadan, as long as they eat nourishing meals at night and before dawn.

Also, after puberty, many Muslim girls start wearing the 'hijab' (headscarf) whenever they go out of their home. In non-Muslim countries this requires particular courage and commitment, as wearing the hijab often attracts adverse comments and bad treatment.

Marriage

Wedding customs differ around the Muslim world. Weddings can take place at home, in a mosque or in a community centre. Some Muslim brides wear local costume and lots of jewellery, while others wear white. A Muslim marriage must be publicly announced and celebrated, and so the occasion may last several days and take place in different locations, with bride and groom needing a variety of outfits.

The actual wedding, the 'nikkah', is simple and can be performed by any Muslim man at any time. There must be two adult male witnesses of good character, plus a 'wali' - the bride's marriage guardian, usually a male relative. A marriage contract will have been prepared. It states that the groom provides 'mahr', a sum of money as a gift, to the bride. If any special conditions have been included in the contract, such as where the couple have agreed to live, these must be announced. The couple accept the contract in front of the witnesses. Some words of advice are spoken, and prayers are said for the happiness of the marriage.

The bridegroom's family give a feast called 'walimah'. Guests bring gifts and wish the couple well. Marriage unites the families of the bride and groom and obliges them to help, advise and support the couple

At a wedding in Tashkent, Uzbekistan.

Hajj

Once in a lifetime, if they have the health and the means, Muslims must make the Hajj - the pilgrimage to Makkah, Mina, Muzdalifah and Arafat.

ON HAJJ

Last year I went on Hajj with my mum and dad and sister. When we first went into the big mosque at Makkah and saw the Ka'bah, we all cried with happiness. We did 'Tawaf', walking round the Ka'bah seven times, and 'Sa'y'. One day we got separated from my dad and it took ages to find him because all the men looked so alike in their ihram.

On the 8th of Dhul Hijjah we went to Mina, five miles outside Makkah, and slept overnight there before setting off for Arafat. Many people walked the whole eight miles, because the roads got jammed with buses. We tried to get close to where the Prophet ﷺ gave his last speech and we spent the day in prayer. On our way back we camped at Muzdalifah, and collected 49 small stones each from the desert.

The 10th was Id day! After praying Fajr, we hurried back to Mina and each threw seven stones at the largest of the three pillars that represent the devils. Everyone cut a lock of hair and some men shaved their heads, and then we went back to Makkah to do Tawaf again. It was a very hectic day! Back in Mina, we changed out of ihram into our ordinary clothes.

On the 11th and again on the 12th we stoned all three pillars. Some people had to be reminded to throw carefully. Then we returned to Makkah.

On Hajj I forgot about everything else – school, home, sport. Being on Hajj put Allah at the centre of everything. When I came back to Munich, all my friends said I had changed. They said I was more kind and not so sarcastic. (Hasan Dyke, Germany, aged 12)

Tents at Mina for pilgrims to live in.

In the past, the journey to Hajj could take months or years. Nowadays pilgrims from all over the world fly to Jeddah and travel on to Makkah. Before leaving, all business must be put in order and each person must make his or her will.

Male pilgrims wear two unsewn pieces of white cloth and many women choose to wear all-white clothes. Everything that pilgrims do on Hajj re-enacts events in the lives of the Prophets Ibrahim, Isma'il and Muhammad (Peace be upon them all). For example, 'Sa'y' means walking seven times between the hills of Safa and Marwah, in memory of how Hajar, the wife of Ibrahim 舒, ran between them, searching for water for her baby son, Isma'il 舒 .

Three stone pillars at Mina represent devils who tried to tempt the Prophet Isma'il 舒 to disobey his father Ibrahim 舒 and Allah. Isma'il 舒 threw stones at the devils, and in remembrance of this, Muslim pilgrims throw stones at the pillars.

Death

When a Muslim is dying, people encourage him or her to say the Shahadah. And when Muslims hear about someone's death they say: 'To Allah we belong and to Him is our return' (Qur'an 2:156).

Muslim graves are dug so that, when the body is placed on its right side, the deceased faces Makkah.

After death, the body is thoroughly washed, not fewer than three times. A man is then shrouded in three pieces of white cloth, and a woman in five. Often the body is taken to a mosque, where the Imam or a knowledgeable person chosen by the family says the funeral prayer. As soon as possible, preferably within twenty-four hours of death, the body is buried. For three days after the burial, and in Turkey and Iran on the seventh and fortieth days, friends bring food to help the sad family and gather in their house to pray and read the Qur'an. This comforts and supports them.

7

THE ISLAMIC YEAR

The most important festivals in the Islamic year are Id ul-Fitr and Id ul-Adha. These were celebrated during the lifetime of the Prophet Muhammad ﷺ. Sunni and Shi'ah Muslims celebrate these festivals.

The chart on the next page shows events that Muslims remember through the year. Sunni Muslims commemorate events which are related in the Qur'an and events in the life of the Prophet Muhammad ﷺ. In addition, Shi'ah Muslims offer special prayers on the dates of birth and death of all the immediate family of the Prophet ﷺ.

A mosque in Malaysia, lit up to celebrate the joyful occasion of Id.

THE BIRTHDAY OF FATIMAH ZAHRAH

Al-Zahrah school in London is named after Fatimah Zahrah, the daughter of the Prophet Muhammad ﷺ. On Yawm al-Zahrah, the birthday of Fatimah Zahrah, the girls of the school put on a special event for their mothers. They sang songs and told stories about Fatimah Zahrah. Many of the songs were in Arabic, but some were in English. A video of the whole celebration was made, to sell to families to raise funds for the school.

One story of Fatimah Zahrah tells of how the Prophet Muhammad ﷺ was praying at the Ka'bah when some men threw rubbish on him. Fatimah stood up to them and told them off, although she was only nine years old. The girls at the London school had written poems about this, saying how much they would like to be like Fatimah.

THE ISLAMIC CALENDAR

Muslims world-wide use a lunar calendar. The months are based on the sighting of the new moon. They are:

Muharram
Safar
Rabi'al-Awwal
Rabi'al-Thani
Jumada al-Awwal
Jumada al-Thani
Rajab
Sha'ban
Ramadan
Shawal
Dhul Qad'ah
Dhul Hijjah

A lunar year is about eleven days shorter than the common 365-day year. Therefore events in the Islamic year move back on this calendar, year by year.

Month and date		Event
Muharram	1	Hijrah (Migration)
	10	Ashura
Rabi' al-Awwal	12-17	Maulid an-Nabi
Jumada al-Awwal	15	The Birthday of Zayn al-Abidin
Jumada al-Thani	20	Yawm al-Zahrah
Rajab	27	Laylat ul-Isra wal Mi'raj
Sha'ban	14-15	Laylat ul-Barat
Ramadan		The month of fasting
	23-27	Laylat ul-Qadr
Shawal	1	Id ul-Fitr
Dhul Hijjah	8-10	The Hajj
	10-12	Id ul-Adha

THE ISLAMIC YEAR

What it Commemorates	What Happens
The Prophet Muhammad ﷺ moves to Madinah, 622 CE, and establishes first Islamic state. Islamic calendar calculated from this date.	Islamic year begins.
The martyrdom of Imam Hussein ؑ at Kerbala in Iraq, 680 CE.	People fast during daylight hours and retell the events.
The birth, life and example of Muhammad ﷺ. Because Sunni and Shi'ah Muslims acknowledge different dates for the birth, 12th and 17th, the week between is used to promote Islamic unity.	People meet to recite Sirah, the Prophet's ﷺ biography, give thanks to Allah for the Prophet ﷺ and his good example, and encourage love for the Prophet ﷺ.
Great grandson of the Prophet ﷺ and son of Imam Hussein ؑ. He wrote a beautiful book of prayers.	
The birthday of Fatimah Zahrah, daughter of the Prophet Muhammad ﷺ and mother of Imam Hussein ؑ. She is known as the leader of women.	Shi'ah Muslims encourage love of Fatimah and the following of her good example with poems and stories about her life. In Iran, this day is also commemorated as women's or mother's day.
The Night Journey of the Prophet Muhammad ﷺ (see page 9).	People make efforts to say extra prayers at night.
The night of promises when Allah decides what will happen to all of His creation in the coming year.	People make extra efforts to pray for forgiveness and in gratitude and hope for the future.
As ordered by Allah in the Qur'an. Gives a special sense of community.	People fast from food, drink and other permitted actions from before dawn to sunset every day for the whole month.
The Night of Power (see page 9). It is a hidden night, looked for in the last ten days of Ramadan.	Extra prayers are said during these nights. People thank Allah for His guidance.
Festival to mark the start of the new month and the end of fasting.	People attend Id prayers at the mosque and give zakah (zakat-ul-Fitr) to ensure everyone can join the festivities. They visit family and friends.
Events in the life of the Prophets Ibrahim, Isma'il and Muhammad (Peace and blessings upon them all) as ordered in the Qur'an.	Muslims must make the Hajj at least once in their life.
The feast of Sacrifice, which is part of the Hajj.	An animal may be sacrificed. People attend Id prayers at the mosque.

Some people do not have to fast. They are the old and frail, and young children, below puberty; people who are ill or recovering from illness; pregnant women and nursing mothers; and people who are travelling from one place to another.

'But if anyone is ill or on a journey, the prescribed period should be made up by days later. Allah intends every facility for you: He does not want to put you to difficulties. [He wants you] to complete the prescribed period and to glorify Him.'
(Qur'an 2: 184)

Ramadan

Ramadan is the ninth month of the Islamic year. It was in Ramadan that the Qur'an was first revealed to Muhammad ﷺ, and it was during this month each year that the revelations were checked.

Ramadan is the month of fasting, ordered by Allah in the Qur'an:

> O you who believe! Fasting is prescribed to you as it was prescribed to those before you that you may learn self-restraint. (Qur'an 2:183)

Each day during the twenty-nine or thirty days of the month, from before dawn until sunset, Muslims fast from food, drink and other normally permitted activities.

RAMADAN IN MADINAH

Muslims from all over the world try to spend Ramadan in Makkah and Madinah, the cities where the Qur'an was revealed. The Prophet's Mosque in Madinah is now one of the largest in the world.

After the sunset call to prayer has been made, everyone breaks their fast. People who have brought dates, fruit and Arabic coffee share them with those near them. People who live in Madinah all the time consider it an honour to bring and share food with their fellow Muslims in this way.

Umar Hegedüs from London has been in Madinah for several Ramadans. He says: 'The atmosphere in the Prophet's Mosque in Ramadan is very special. You feel very close to the Muslim Ummah and to the ideals of sharing which began with the first Islamic community.'

They feel hungry and thirsty, but most Muslims enjoy Ramadan because it brings the community together in a positive way. Someone who is fasting in the heat of west Africa knows that other Muslims in cold places like Finland and western China are fasting too. Fasting reminds people of how they are dependent on Allah and so it gives them greater 'taqwa' (consciousness of Allah).

Praying behind the Sheikh in Ramadan, Peckham.

RAMADAN IN LONDON

The Yeni Peckham Cami, the New Peckham Mosque, is a complete contrast with the Prophet's Mosque in Madinah. It is a converted church building. But here too members of the local Muslim community share their meals with visitors from overseas. Every year in Ramadan, the Turkish-run mosque is host to Sheikh Muhammad Nazim, a Sufi Sheikh (see Glossary). He comes to help Muslims living in a non-Muslim country to observe all the practices of Ramadan. He is a well-known and respected teacher, and so his pupils ('murids') come from all over the world to spend Ramadan with him. Every afternoon, when it is most difficult to fast, Sheikh Nazim talks to his murids. He teaches them that, wherever they are from - Malaysia, Canada, Germany, Australia, Pakistan, Scotland, Cyprus, or France - they are all one Ummah; and the teachings of the Qur'an can be practised wherever they live.

It was a custom in Egypt to use special lamps to light the way to the mosque for night prayers. Now they are often carried by children, as part of the fun of Ramadan.

Glossary

adhan   call to prayer, made five times a day from the mosque, in the home, or wherever people make salah.

Allah   The Islamic name for the One True God, in the Arabic language. Used in preference to the word God, the term has no plural and no gender characteristics.

Hajj   annual pilgrimage to Makkah, in the month of Dhul Hijjah, which each Muslim must undertake at least once in a lifetime. A Muslim male who has completed Hajj is called Hajji (feminine: Hajjah). See also 'Umrah'.

halal   any action which is permitted or lawful.

haram   anything unlawful or forbidden.

hijab   literally, 'curtain' or 'veil'; often used to describe the headscarf or modest dress for women, who must cover everything except their face and hands when in the sight of anyone other than their immediate family.

Hijrah   the emigration of the Prophet Muhammad ﷺ from Makkah to Madinah in 622 CE.

Id   literally, 'recurring happiness'; a religious holiday for thanking Allah and celebrating a happy occasion.

Id ul-Adha   celebration of the Sacrifice – commemorating the Prophet Ibrahim's willingness to sacrifice his son Isma'il for Allah (Peace be upon them).

Id ul-Fitr   celebration of breaking the fast on the day after Ramadan ends, the 1st of Shawal, the tenth Islamic month.

ihram   1. the state or condition Muslims enter into, to perform Hajj and Umrah. Many normally permitted actions are placed out of bounds.

2. the name of the two plain white unsewn cloths worn by male pilgrims, indicating brotherhood, equality and purity. For women the dress of ihram consists of their normal modest clothing.

Imam   literally, 'leader'; a person who leads communal prayer or a founder of an Islamic school of law. In Shi'ah Islam, Imam is also the title of Ali ﷺ and his successors.

iqamah   call to stand up for salah.

Islam   peace attained through willing obedience to Allah's divine guidance.

khutbah   speech made on special occasions such as the Friday and Id prayers.

minbar   platform from which the Imam delivers the khutbah in the mosque or praying ground.

Muhammad ﷺ   literally, 'praised'; the name of the final Prophet ﷺ.

Muslim   one who claims to have accepted Islam by professing the Shahadah.

salah   prescribed communication with and worship of Allah, performed under specific conditions, in the manner taught by the Prophet Muhammad ﷺ and recited in the Arabic language. The five daily times of salah are fixed by Allah.

sawm	fasting from just before dawn until sunset. Abstinence is required from all food and drink (including water), smoking and conjugal relations.
Shahadah	declaration of faith which consists of the statement: 'There is no god except Allah and Muhammad is the Messenger of Allah.'
Shari'ah	Islamic law based on the Qur'an and Sunnah.
Sheikh	a respected person who knows a great deal about Islam and about how to lead a good life and teaches these things to others.
Sirah	biographical writings about the conduct and example of the Prophet Muhammad 變.
Sufi	a Muslim who tries to become closer to Allah. Sometimes Muslims do this by meeting to recite the Qur'an and the names of Allah. Both Sunni and Shi'ah Muslims can follow the Sufi path.
Tawaf	walking seven times round the Ka'bah in worship of Allah. A part of Hajj and Umrah.
Ummah	the world-wide Muslim community.
Umrah	the lesser pilgrimage to Makkah which can be performed at any time of year.
wudu	washing before salah.
zakah	purification of wealth by payment of an annual welfare tax. This is an obligatory act of worship. The zakah is used to help people in need.
Zakat-ul-Fitr	welfare payment given before the end of Ramadan.

Book List

The Qur'an
Most of the extracts from the Qur'an used in this book are taken from the English translation and commentary by Abdullah Yusuf Ali. Many Muslims think that the style and choice of words of his translation make it close in meaning to the original words revealed to the Prophet Muhammad 變 . Yusuf Ali worked for many years translating and giving helpful explanations of difficult passages. His work was published in thirty installments from 1934 to 1937.

Hegedüs, Umar, *The Mosque*, A. and C. Black, 1996

Khattab, Huda, *Stories from the Muslim World*, Macdonald, 1987

Knight, Khadijah, *Islamic Festivals*, Heinemann, 1995

Lewis, Bernard (Ed.), *The World of Islam*, Thames and Hudson, 1992

Matar, N. I., *Islam for Beginners*, Writers and Readers Publishing, Inc., 1992

Nasr, Seyyed Hossein, *A Young Muslim's Guide to the Modern World*, Islamic Text Society, 1993

Sardar, Ziauddin and Malik, Zafar Abbas, *Muhammad for beginners*, Icon Books, 1994

Sarwar, Ghulam, *Islam. Beliefs and teachings*, Muslim Educational Trust, 1993

Islam Source Book for Schools, United by Faith, 1996 (Reference and issue-based material, up-to-date biographies to meet agreed syllabus requirements from SCAA's Faith Working Groups. Available from ICIS, see page 2.)

Subhanallah – The Wonders of Creation in the Holy Qur'an, The World Federation of Khoja Shia Ithna-Asheri Muslim Communities, 1993 (Well-illustrated source book of sections from the Qur'an related to people, animals and the natural world. Available from ICIS, see page 2.)

Note on Dates

Each religion has its own system for counting the years of its history. The starting point may be related to the birth or death of a special person or an important event. In everyday life, today, when different communities have dealings with each other, they need to use the same counting system for setting dates in the future and writing accounts of the past. The Western system is now used throughout the world. It is based on Christian beliefs about Jesus: AD (Anno Domini = in the year of our Lord) and BC (Before Christ). Members of the various world faiths use the common Western system, but, instead of AD and BC, they say and write CE (in the Common Era) and BCE (before the Common Era).

Index